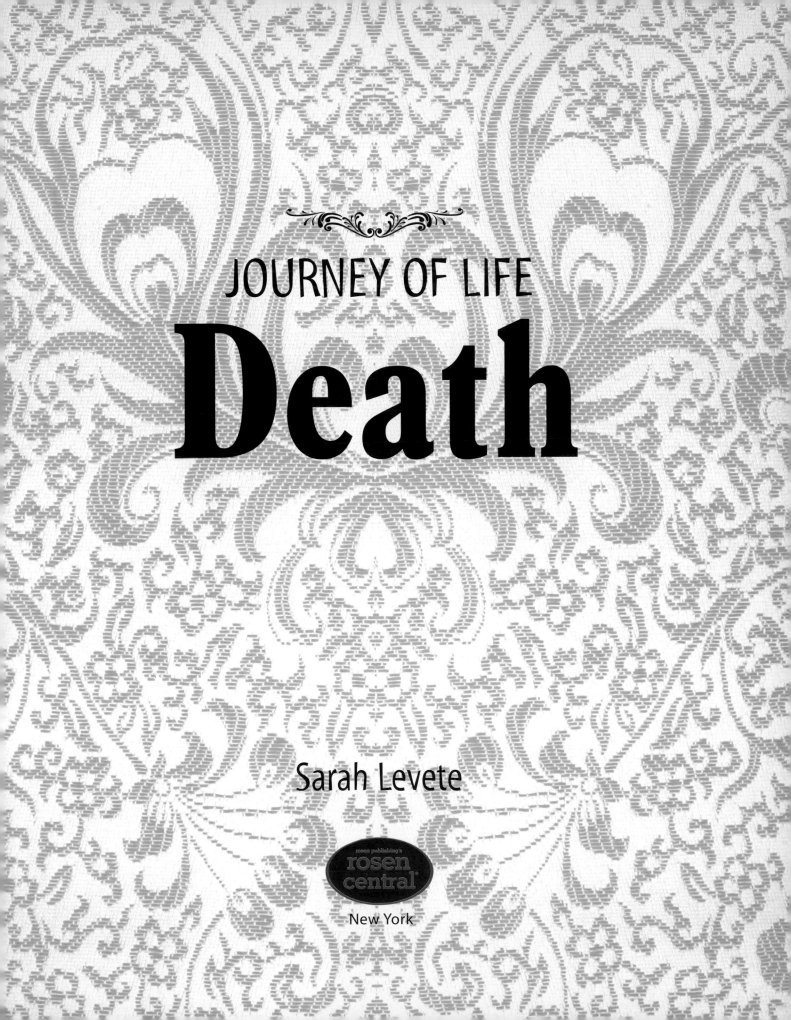

JOURNEY OF LIFE
Death

Sarah Levete

rosen publishing's
rosen
central

New York

Published in 2010 by The Rosen Publishing Group Inc.
29 East 21st Street, New York, NY 10010

First Edition

Design: Paul Myerscough and Emma DeBanks
Editor: Sarah Eason
Editor for Wayland: Katie Powell
Picture research: Maria Joannou
Consultant: Sue Happs

Library of Congress Cataloging-in-Publication Data

Levete, Sarah.
  Death / Sarah Levete. – 1st ed.
    p. cm. – (Journey of life)
  Includes index.
  ISBN 978-1-4358-5351-5 (library binding)
  ISBN 978-1-4358-5456-7 (paperback)
  ISBN 978-1-4358-5457-4 (6-pack)
  1. Funeral service. 2. Funeral rites and ceremonies. 3. Death–
Religious aspects. I. Title.
  BL619.F85L48 2010
  203'.88–dc22

                                          2008052890

Picture Acknowledgements:
Alamy Images p. 18 (Ami Vitale), p. 22 (Frances Roberts), p. 26 (imagebroker), p. 40 (Nick Greaves), p. 31 (Sally and
Richard Greenhill), pp. 6, 8 (Steve Skjold), p. 21 (World Religions Photo Library); **Art Directors & Trip** p. 34; **Corbis**
p. 14 (Andrew Lichtenstein), p. 28 (Christophe Boisvieux), p. 19 (Farooq Khan/EPA), p. 29 (Joseph Khakshouri), p. 37
(Owen Franken), pp. 15, 36 (Reuters); **Dreamstime** pp. 24, 43; **Getty Images** p. 33 (Raveendran/AFP), p. 16 (Sean
Gallup), p. 41 (Stock4B), pp. 13, 32 (Stringer/AFP); **Istockphoto** pp. 4, 7, 9, 10, 17, 23, 27, 35; **Photolibrary** p. 5
(Imagestate), p. 25 (Paul Nevin); **Photos.com** p. 11; **Shutterstock** pp. 12, 20, 38, 39.

Cover photograph: **Corbis** (Anne Griffiths Belt)

Manufactured in China

Contents

What is death?

From flowers to human beings, every living thing eventually dies. Death is one stage in the journey of life. Some people believe that death is the end of that journey. Others believe that there is some kind of life after death.

We cannot know for sure what happens after a person dies. The death of a friend or relative is a very sad time, and people miss their loved one. Rites and rituals often help the living to cope with their loss, and with the unknown of death. For centuries, people have observed rites and rituals to remember and honor the dead. Some of these are connected to religious beliefs, and others relate to customs that have grown up around particular societies.

When a person dies, the body begins to decay. It is either buried or cremated (burned to ashes). The ancient Egyptians believed that a person's soul was reunited with its body in the afterlife. To preserve the body for the afterlife, they embalmed or mummified the bodies of important people, drying them out and wrapping them in bandages. The bodies were buried in tombs, together with goods they would need in the next world, such as furniture and food.

The terra cotta warrior sculptures found in China were created by a Chinese emperor, Shi Huangdi. They were buried with the emperor after his death to help him rule in the afterlife.

In 1974, a Chinese farmer came across an incredible archeological find by chance— a massive burial complex with an "army" of over 7,000 terra cotta sculptures of warriors. The burial site was made for China's first emperor, who lived from 259 to 210 BCE. The pottery soldiers were buried with the emperor so that they could serve him in the afterlife.

Today, some cultures and religions, including many Christians, embalm corpses, but not by wrapping them in bandages. Modern embalming is done using chemicals.

A body is usually embalmed to make it look more lifelike. This can help grieving relatives feel more comfortable when they view the body. Embalming also preserves the body for a short while before a burial ceremony.

Religious or spiritual beliefs about death are often closely linked to ideas about life. Some people believe that we have a spirit or soul that travels to another realm, or world, after death. Others think that the body is resurrected and used again in an afterlife.

This book looks at how six major religions respond to death, from the practical issues to ceremonies that mark the passing of life. It also looks at the responses of some other beliefs and cultures.

FOCUS ON:
Historical rites

Many archaeological discoveries of ancient societies have uncovered burial sites and funeral mounds. The remains of an early Neanderthal man who lived in about 60,000 BCE were found with animal antlers and flower fragments. This suggests that earliest man offered gifts with the dead and performed certain rites to mark death. After death, the bodies of Viking chieftains were often placed in ships with their tools and weapons. The ships were set on fire as they were sent out to sea. Often, these rituals were only observed for the powerful or wealthy members of a society. The bodies of ordinary people might end up in an unmarked grave or be burned without ceremony.

Preparing for a funeral

*A*cross the world, there are several branches of Christianity. The main groups are Roman Catholic, Orthodox, and Protestant, but within them there are many more denominations. The denominations share the same core Christian beliefs, but they place different emphasis on certain aspects of them. This variety is reflected in the range of Christian rituals that mark death. Christian funerals may vary according to the denomination and the country in which the funeral is held.

In medieval Europe, the bodies of poor people were disposed of rapidly and with little ceremony. People thought that bodies carried infectious diseases. Priests probably offered little support to the bereaved. Today, a priest may offer support to a dying person and his or her relatives. Sometimes the priest offers the last rites to a dying person. He, or sometimes she, says prayers and invites the person who is dying to repent for their sins. The person who is dying may also take Holy Communion.

Today, in many Western countries, most of the practical arrangements that follow a death are organized by an undertaker at a funeral home. After discussion with the relatives, the undertaker takes on responsibility for most aspects of the funeral. The family choose a coffin and decide on the funeral service and how the person will be buried. The undertaker embalms the body, often dressing it in the deceased's finest clothes.

Viewing the body of the deceased at a funeral home gives friends and relatives the opportunity to come to terms with the death, and prepare for the funeral to come.

FOCUS ON:
The cross

Jesus Christ, who Christians believe was the son of God, rose from death on the third day after he was crucified. This is called the resurrection. The death and resurrection of Jesus Christ lie at the heart of Christianity. The symbol of Christianity, the cross, is a symbol of Jesus Christ's death on the cross. The crucifix with Christ on it reminds Christians of his death and sacrifice; the empty cross reminds them of the resurrection.

Sometimes, relatives put special objects in the coffin. At the funeral home, relatives can view the body in an open coffin and say their private goodbyes.

The funeral usually takes place a few days after death. The body is often taken to the funeral ceremony in a car called a hearse.

Traditionally, Roman Catholics gather at the deceased's home or the funeral home to pray for that person's soul before the funeral. This is called a wake. Friends and family come together to offer support and comfort. A priest leads the wake and relatives may give a eulogy, or speech.

When a Christian takes Holy Communion, also called the *Eucharist* or *Mass*, he or she eats a small piece of bread or a wafer and sips some wine. The bread symbolizes Christ's body, and the wine symbolizes his blood. This rite reminds Christians of Christ's sacrifice.

The funeral service

A Christian funeral is an opportunity for family and friends to grieve for their loss. It is also a time to mark the passing of the soul from the physical body to eternal life, a key Christian belief. The funeral service reminds the living of Christ's resurrection and of God's presence. It gives support to family and friends as the community comes together to pray for the soul of the deceased. Christians believe that the power of prayer can help the souls of the dead pass toward God.

People often send flowers to a funeral, sometimes in the form of a circular wreath. This represents the continuity of life after death. It is traditional to wear dark colors or black to a funeral, although more recently people have worn bright colors to celebrate the life of the deceased.

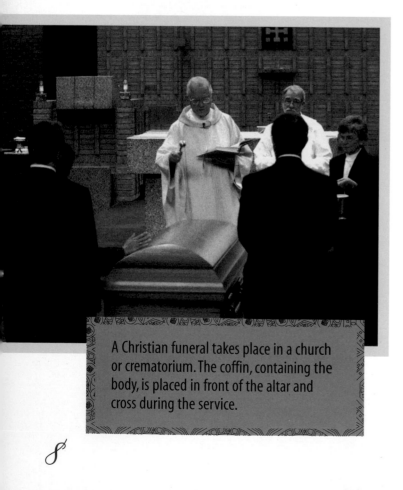

A Christian funeral takes place in a church or crematorium. The coffin, containing the body, is placed in front of the altar and cross during the service.

Many Christian funerals are now personalized. A priest or minister leads the service and prayers in a church. A relative or friend may give a speech about the person who has died. There may be readings of that person's favorite poems or recordings of their favorite music, from classical to pop.

Roman Catholic funeral services may include the Holy Communion service that symbolizes the Last Supper that Jesus Christ shared with his disciples before his death. The focus of this service is prayer and remembrance of Christ's sacrifice.

Christians are buried in consecrated ground, in a cemetery or sometimes in a churchyard. The burial, or committal, is a particularly emotional moment. Around the grave, the priest or minister leads a brief service and prayers.

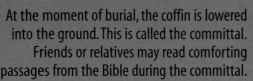

Some time after the burial, a tombstone is placed at the head of the grave. This stone is engraved with the person's name, dates of birth and death, and sometimes a few words of remembrance, or an epitaph. This can be either religious or a simple message such as "Gone but not forgotten."

Different styles of funeral have developed in Christian communities around the world. In New Orleans, some African-American funerals feature a march from the home or church of the deceased to the cemetery with friends, family, and a jazz band. At first, the music is serious and somber, but after the burial, the march continues with lively, joyful music.

Today, many Christians choose cremation instead of burial. It was only in the last century that the Roman Catholic Church began to allow this, since many Catholics believed that destroying a body by burning it was against the Christian teachings on the resurrection of the body at the Day of Judgement. Some Eastern Orthodox denominations of Christianity (practiced mainly in eastern European countries) still forbid cremation. They believe that the body must be kept for resurrection on the Day of Judgement, when Jesus will return to Earth and judge the good and the bad.

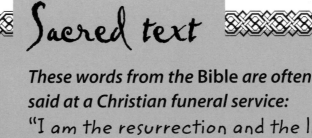

Sacred text

These words from the Bible are often said at a Christian funeral service:
"I am the resurrection and the life," says the Lord; "he that believes in me, though he were dead, yet shall he live: and whoever lives and believes in me shall never die."
From the **New Testament, John 11:25-26**

Mourning and the afterlife

*I*n Christian traditions, friends and family gather at a small reception after the funeral. Like the Roman Catholic gathering before a funeral, this is also called a wake. It is another opportunity to remember the deceased.

If a person has been cremated, their ashes may be buried in a cemetery or churchyard, scattered in a place of significance, or kept in a special urn. Roman Catholics only allow the ashes to be buried, not scattered.

The anniversary of the death may be marked with a visit to the grave, and the saying of special prayers in church.

In the nineteenth century, the formal mourning period for a deceased relative could last for several months, or even years. The family withdrew from society and wore only black. The deaths of thousands of men across Europe during World War I put an end to these very long mourning periods. Today, in many Christian communities there is little formal mourning.

Christians believe that life's journey does not end with death. The physical body decays but the person's spirit or soul lives on. Christ's resurrection brought the hope of eternal life to all Christians. Christian souls pass either to heaven, a place of paradise, or to hell, a place of torment. In both places they have eternal life. Christians believe that Christ sacrificed himself to forgive the sins of others, and that his resurrection proves that death cannot defeat the power of God and love.

Christians believe that if people repent of their sins in their earthly life, they can pass to heaven after death. This belief in an afterlife influences the way a person lives their life on Earth.

This Christian image of heaven and hell was painted in the 15th century. At that time, all Christians believed that heaven and hell were physical places a person went to when they died.

There are many Christian ideas about heaven and hell. Today, some Christians still believe heaven and hell are actual physical places, but others think of them more as states of being.

Roman Catholics believe that most people pass to an in-between place called purgatory before they can reach heaven. Jehovah's Witnesses, a group of Christians who believe that Jesus will return to Earth very soon, believe there is no hell. They say the souls of the wicked will be destroyed on the Day of Judgement, and when Christ returns to Earth to pass judgement on men, only Jehovah's Witnesses will be saved.

MODERN DEBATE:
CREMATION IN GREECE

Athens, the capital city of Greece, is running out of burial sites. The Greek Eastern Orthodox Church refuses to allow cremation. Many people have to rent a burial plot just for three years. After this time, they must remove the body, now just bones, and place them in a special building. The Greek government recently introduced a law that allows cremation for people who are not members of the Greek Orthodox Church. The Church thinks that this undermines their authority, and the traditional values and identity of its people. The government argues that cremation is a practical necessity, and that the Church must accept that Greece is a multicultural country, where people of other faiths cremate their dead.

Do you think some bodies should be cremated in Athens, or should the views of the Church outweigh practical considerations?

Preparing a body for burial

*J*ews, the people who follow the faith called Judaism, have settled all over the world. There are several traditions or movements within Judaism, including Orthodox and Liberal Judaism, and they may practice variations on the basic funeral rites described below. For Jews, death is a natural process in which the body returns to the earth. The rites around death reflect this.

When a person is dying, family members gather together. If possible, the dying person recites the *Shema*, an important Jewish prayer that is a declaration of faith, starting with the words: "Hear O Israel, the Lord our God, the Lord is One." (Deuteronomy 6:4–9). The dying person confesses his or her sins. At death, their eyes are closed. A lit candle symbolizes the person's soul.

It is considered an honor to prepare the body for burial. It must be treated with absolute respect. Traditionally, this is done by a special group of volunteers, members of a group called the *chevra kaddisha* (holy society). Preparing the body for burial is considered a very holy task, and an act of selfless love because the deceased cannot offer thanks for it.

Men prepare the bodies of men, and women prepare the bodies of women. The body is washed with warm water, then dressed in simple white shrouds called *tachrichim*.

This man is praying in his prayer shawl, or *tallith*. Jews are buried in their prayer shawls, with one of the shawl's tassels cut off. This symbolizes that the dead person can no longer use it.

Sometimes a group of men will sit with the body until burial, to watch over it. The men are called *shomrim* (watchers).

FOCUS ON:
Chevra kaddisha

A relative or a member of the chevra kaddisha sits with the body at all times, sometimes reading from the Psalms. The Psalms are songs which form one of the Jewish holy books. People sitting with the body are not allowed to eat or drink because this would not be respectful to the dead. They must wash and cleanse themselves afterward.

In the Jewish faith, embalming is not allowed because it interferes with the natural decay of the body. However, a rabbi (spiritual leader of Judaism) can make special allowances for autopsies (examinations to find out how a person died) or organ donation.

On hearing of the death of a close relative, a person is known as an *onan*. This means an immediate mourner, such as a husband or wife, child, brother, or sister. The onan is responsible for making sure that the burial takes place as soon as possible. In times when Jewish families lived in communities near each other, it was possible for family members to come together within a day (by sundown) to bury the dead.

Today, Jewish family members may live all over the world, so it often takes time for everyone to travel home for the burial. Still, the burial often takes place within two days of death. However, burials are not allowed on the Jewish holy day, called the Sabbath.

Returning to the earth

*I*n Israel, the Jewish homeland, Jews are buried without a coffin so that the body returns to the earth more quickly. In other parts of the world, local laws state that coffins must be used. Then simple coffins are made only from wood, which decomposes easily.

Jewish burial customs follow a simple format. There are few decisions for the relatives to make. For instance, all Jews, whether rich or poor, wear similar shrouds and are buried in simple pine coffins. This shows that all people are equal in death.

Attending a funeral is a religious duty in Judaism. Jews tear a piece of their clothing to symbolize the tear in their heart. Liberal Jews wear a black ribbon instead and tear this. People of other faiths attending the ceremony are not allowed to wear symbols of their religion, such as a crucifix. There are no flowers at an Orthodox Jewish funeral because they wither and die; giving a donation to a charity is considered a more worthwhile way to remember the person. A simple ceremony takes place in the funeral home, synagogue, or near the graveside. A rabbi recites psalms and prayers. The coffin, or the shrouded body, is carried to the grave in a Jewish cemetery. As the men carry the coffin, they pause seven times to reflect on how hard it is for the living to part with the dead. During this time, they recite part of *Psalm 91* at each pause (see box on page 15).

Jewish mourners place soil on the coffin. If possible, soil from Israel, the Jewish homeland, is thrown over the coffin.

A Jewish relative expresses his grief at a funeral service. Traditionally, Jews wear dark clothing to a funeral, such as the black suits and hats worn by the men in this photograph. Women wear head coverings.

FOCUS ON:
Dust to dust

"For dust you are and to dust you shall return," God told Adam, the first man on Earth, as told in the Jewish holy books. This belief influences the Jewish death ritual, which quickly returns the body to the soil.

If a coffin is used, holes are drilled into the sides so that the body is in close contact with the soil. Mourners throw a handful of soil onto the coffin.

After the burial, friends stand in two rows through which the close family walk, to receive words of comfort and support. Traditionally, mourners ritually wash their hands after the burial.

Sacred text

1) For
2) For His angels
3) For His angels He will order
4) For His angels He will order for you
5) For His angels He will order for you to guard you
6) For His angels He will order for you to guard you in all
7) For His angels He will order for you to guard you in all your ways

Psalm 91.11 *as recited at some Jewish burials*

Mourning a loved one

After the burial, the mourners and close community gather together for a meal called *seudat havra'ah*. Family and friends console each other at the gathering and eat food that is round in shape, such as bagels, lentils, and hard-boiled eggs. The roundness of the food symbolizes the circle of life (birth, life, and death) and the eternal nature of the soul.

Candles are lit both after death and on the anniversary of the death. They burn for seven days after the death of a loved one, and for 24 hours on the anniversary date.

Jewish mourning is traditionally divided into several stages of seven days, one month, and finally 11 months. For seven days, a candle burns. Each day, close relatives recite a special prayer called *kaddish*. Mourners do not cut their hair or shave. They sit on low stools; this shows they have been brought low by suffering.

After three days, the family can receive visitors, who usually bring food. At this time, the local Jewish community can offer words of comfort and support. This mourning period allows the family to grieve together and then to move on with their everyday lives.

After a month, mourners return to work or school, but they must avoid entertainment and pleasure. They continue to recite the kaddish each day. After 11 months, life returns to normal. In many Jewish communities, however, the mourning period may be shorter. Sometime between the first week of mourning and the first anniversary of death, relatives mark the grave with a simple tombstone.

FOCUS ON:
Remembering the Holocaust

Yom Hashoah is the official day on which Jews remember the Holocaust, the persecution of Jews in World War II (1939–1945). Ceremonies include the lighting of candles and prayers for the victims of the Holocaust. Throughout Israel, a siren sounds for two minutes. People stop work while they remember the millions who were killed.

On the anniversary of a death, pebbles are sometimes left on the grave. There are different ideas about the significance of these, but some people believe they stand for the everlasting nature of the soul.

The anniversary of a loved one's death is called *yarzheit*. Relatives visit the grave, light a candle, and attend a synagogue service to recite kaddish. For the rest of their lives, close relatives will light a candle and say the kaddish or yarzheit.

Although Jews believe in an afterlife, the emphasis in Judaism is on the actions and life of the living. Liberal Jews believe that the soul is immortal and returns to God. They do not believe in bodily resurrection or physical life after death, so cremation is allowed. Orthodox Jews believe in a physical and spiritual life after death when the Messiah (a king sent from God at the end of time) will come to Earth and to the land of Israel to judge humankind.

Preparing for death

*L*ife on Earth is an opportunity for Muslims, the followers of Islam, to prove their commitment to Allah, or God. Muslims live life to honor Allah and to prepare for his judgement in death. The rites to prepare a Muslim for the afterlife come from the *Hadith*, the traditional teachings of the prophet Muhammad (pbuh). These rites form part of *Shari'ah*, or Muslim law.

Friends and family gather at the bedside of a dying Muslim. He or she can ask for forgiveness for any sins and repeats the *Shahadah* (others recite it if the person is unable to do this). The Shahadah is the declaration of faith in Allah: "There is no God but Allah and

This group of women have gathered to listen to readings from the Qur'an following the death of a relative.

Muhammad (pbuh) is His messenger." These are the first words a newborn baby hears; these are the last words a Muslim hears before death. When a Muslim dies, the eyes are gently closed. Relatives inform the imam, or spiritual leader, and he comes to the house and recites prayers from the Qur'an (or Koran), the Islamic holy book, over the body.

There is a detailed ritual to prepare the body for burial. Relatives or elders of the Muslim community prepare the body. Men prepare men's bodies, and women prepare women's bodies. First, the body is washed. The right hand is washed three times, then the left hand is washed three times.

Mourners carry the shrouded body to a mosque for prayers.

The mouth is rinsed three times and then cleaned with a cloth. The wrists to elbows are washed. Finally, the left foot is washed three times, followed by the right foot. The body is then dried.

Sometimes, the body is anointed with a sweet-smelling spice called camphor. It is wrapped in a white shroud called a *kafan*. This is usually made up of three pieces of material for men, and five pieces for women. Wrapping the body in a simple cloth shows that all people are equal before Allah in death, regardless of their wealth or status on Earth.

It is expected that friends and family will weep and grieve over the loss of a loved one, but noisy or extreme shows of grief such as wailing are not encouraged. Muslims believe that Allah gives and takes life, so it is inappropriate to cry about this.

FOCUS ON:
Burial

Burial must be carried out as soon as possible, usually within 24 hours of death. This is to free the soul from the physical body, and to make sure that the body does not start to decay before burial.

Equality in death

A Muslim funeral is a simple, modest ceremony. This reflects the Muslim belief that all people are equal in death. Islam does not allow cremation. The Qur'an emphasizes that at the Last Judgement, Allah will raise the dead to life. Muslims also believe that a person's body was given by Allah and it must be returned.

Once the ritual preparation of the body has taken place, prayers are said, often at the house of the deceased. The mourners, usually wearing white, carry the body to the place of burial. The mourners walk in silence to the graveside. If possible, the body is buried without a coffin, to ensure maximum contact with the soil.

All Muslims are buried with their body facing the right side, so that it is turned toward Makkah (Mecca), the holy city.

MODERN DEBATE:
ADAPTING TO OTHER CUSTOMS AND LAWS

Today, Muslims live all over the world, sometimes in countries that do not follow Islamic law and where another religion, or no religion, is dominant. Burial practices there may differ from the rituals laid down in Shari'ah law. For example, it may not be possible for Muslims to bury the dead without a coffin, or to refuse an autopsy. Under Islamic law, autopsies are not allowed. If death occurs during the weekend, it may not be possible to bury the dead within 24 hours. These issues raise the question of whether Muslims should adapt to the laws of the country where they are living, or whether the laws of the country should honor Muslim practices.

What do you think?

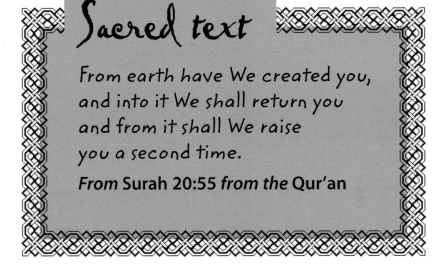

A prayer leader faces Makkah, with the body of the deceased in front of him. Behind him are rows of mourners, who also face Makkah as prayers for the deceased are said.

FOCUS ON:
Angels

According to Islamic faith, each person has two angels, called Munkar and Nakir, who are messengers from Allah. They are always present, even though they cannot be seen. After the burial, the mourners turn away from the grave. The two angels then come to ask the deceased questions about his or her faith. The mourners pray at this time to help the deceased answer the questions.

In some Islamic traditions, women do not attend the graveside, even if the deceased is a female relative. Mourners form rows facing the direction of Makkah, with the prayer leader and the body in front of them. Prayers by the graveside are said standing. Usually, Muslim prayers are said in the prostration position, with the forehead, nose, palms, knees, and toes touching the floor.

The grave is positioned so that the buried body can face Makkah. Relatives throw three handfuls of soil into the grave, reciting prayers as they do so. Many of the prayers are said in silence. Friends comfort the family but encourage them to accept the will of Allah.

Mourning and the afterlife

After burial, there is a usually a three-day mourning period, marked by increased devotion and worship to Allah. Visitors come to the house, bringing food, offering words of comfort and reminding relatives that the death is Allah's will. Prayers are said almost continuously. After three days, the mourning stops. However, in some parts of the world, widows stay at home for four months and ten days.

Muslim women express their grief. During mourning, Muslim women do not wear jewelry or makeup.

The family is responsible for paying off any debts left by the relative who died. They are also expected to keep in contact with other family members and friends of the deceased. They frequently visit the grave to remember the individual and to remind themselves of the Last Judgement, at which everyone will be called to account. Muslims believe that life on Earth is only a stage in a person's journey. Death is the gateway to eternal life.

The time between death and the Last Judgement is called *barzakh*. Dead souls "sleep" in their graves, waiting for judgement. Those going to hell begin to suffer in the grave. On the Last Judgement, each person stands before Allah.

Azrail is the Islamic Angel of Death. He has a book in which he writes the names of those who are born, and then erases the names of those who die. Israfil is the Angel who will announce the Last Judgement. He separates souls from their bodies.

A plain tombstone marks a Muslim grave, which is raised above the ground to discourage people from walking on it.

Muslims who have lived according to the Islamic code can reach paradise, a place like a garden. Those who have not, will go to hell. There is no "in-between" realm. After death, there is no chance of forgiveness. Others cannot "save" the soul of someone else with their prayers.

Souls who gain entry to paradise walk on a narrow bridge over hell. Souls destined for hell fall off the bridge, weighed down by their sins.

During Id-ul-Fitr, a Muslim festival that marks the end of the fasting period called Ramadan, families visit the graves of loved ones to say prayers. This visit also reminds them of the temporary nature of life, and of the importance of living according to Muslim principles to achieve eternal life.

FOCUS ON:
Heaven and hell

Entry to paradise or hell depends on the way a person lived on Earth. A Muslim who lived according to the will of Allah will have followed the five main beliefs, or pillars, of Islam:

- affirming faith daily
- praying five times a day
- helping the poor and needy
- fasting during Ramadan
- going on *Hajj*, a pilgrimage to Makkah (Mecca)

Releasing a soul

*I*t is a Hindu duty, or *dharma*, to honor the rites of death. Death is one of the 16 *samskars*, or rites of passage. This samskar is important because it influences what happens to a person's soul (*atman*) in another world. Different countries, villages, and communities observe this samskar in slightly different ways.

When a Hindu is dying, relatives gather around and help prepare the individual for death. They burn incense and place a lit lamp near the person's head. They sit together, chant, and recite prayers and writings from the Vedas, the Hindu scriptures. Traditionally, the body must be cremated within 24 hours of death.

Hindus believe that if they die in the Indian city of Varanasi, also called Benares, on the shores of the holy River Ganges, they can speed up the process of *moksha*. Moksha is release from the continuous cycle of birth, death, and rebirth to which all souls are chained. When a Hindu does not die near the Ganges, families often arrange to sprinkle his or her ashes in that river's holy waters.

Varanasi is by the River Ganges. The River Ganges is sacred to Hindus— dying near it is believed to help a person's soul pass to heaven.

According to Hindu belief, when the body dies, it must let go of the soul so that the soul can continue its journey into other realms. The body is of no use now; it is like an empty shell. It is also considered impure, so Hindus perform several rituals to cleanse it and to speed up the soul's release.

Close relatives bathe the body, then dress it in the person's finest clothes. Jewelry, such as the *mangal sutra* (which was tied around a bride's neck when she married) is sometimes left on the body. Traditionally, the relatives drop some holy water from the Ganges on the person's head and place a few leaves from the holy basil plant, *tulsi*, next to the body. The tulsi is linked to Vishnu, a Hindu god, protector of the universe. The tulsi is believed to have great healing powers.

The family place the body on a mat on the floor. They arrange garlands of colorful flowers, such as roses, jasmine, marigolds, and sweet-smelling sandalwood, around it. In some traditions, some puffed rice (*pinda*) is placed in the mouth of the deceased, to provide nourishment for the spiritual journey ahead.

In India, relatives usually carry the body on a bamboo stretcher or on a cart pulled by animals. In other countries, the body is usually taken in a hearse. The procession often passes places that were memorable to the person who died.

In India, the body is often taken to a funeral pyre, but in many other countries, the body, which must be in a coffin, is taken to a crematorium.

Cremating a body by the holy River Ganges is also thought to help the deceased's soul pass on.

FOCUS ON:
Samskar

There are 16 important stages, or samskars, in a Hindu's life, each one marked by different rituals and ceremonies. It is a religious duty to observe the samskars. Other samskars include the birth of a baby, a child's first haircut, and marriage.

The cremation ceremony

he flames of a cremation fire represent Brahma, the Hindu god responsible for creative power. Cremation frees the soul quickly from the physical body.

Mourners say prayers for the deceased as the cremation takes place.

According to Hindu belief, a human is made up of five elements: fire, earth, water, air, and a spiritual element. The first four elements come from the Earth. The fifth comes from a higher realm. When a person is cremated, the four elements return to their Earthly origin. The fifth element travels to the higher world with the soul, where it continues its journey in the cycle of life (birth, old age, death, and rebirth).

Only young children and holy men or women are buried. They are believed to be pure, so there is no need for the purification of cremation.

When cremation takes place on a pyre, the chief mourner, who is usually the eldest son, or a Brahmin (a member of the priestly caste or group) circles the pyre three times with the body, walking anticlockwise. This symbolizes that things go backward at death, because during normal worship, people circle a shrine clockwise.

Sacred text

O Supreme light, lead us from untruth to truth, from darkness to light, and from death to immortality.

A Vedic prayer

MODERN DEBATE:
FUNERAL PYRE OR CREMATORIUM?

In India, the birthplace of Hinduism, a huge amount of wood is used every day to cremate the dead. Many people are worried about the effect of this on the environment. Forests are cut down for the wood, but supplies are running out. In addition, the ashes of the dead, scattered in holy rivers, are clogging up the flowing waters. The Indian government has built lots of electrically powered crematoria, but many Hindus still choose the traditional funeral pyre. Watching the flames leap high into the air reassures mourners that the soul of a loved one is rising to heaven. They may also be reluctant to use a crematorium because if the power supply is interrupted, the cremation will be affected. Is it better to protect the environment in the long-term, or to honor this traditional religious practice?

Hindus believe that the flames from the funeral pyre help separate the soul from the physical body and speed up its release to heaven.

Then the body is placed on a ghat or platform. The chief mourner prays for the departing soul and lights the pyre with a flame. He throws ghee (liquid butter) on to the fire to make the flames burn fiercely.

The cremation marks the beginning of mourning. On a funeral pyre, it takes a few hours for the fire to consume the body. After this, the mourners return home. Some male relatives return later to collects the ashes. These are scattered in a river or, if possible, in the waters of the sacred Ganges.

Death and reincarnation

After the cremation, family and friends wash and change to cleanse themselves. Then they return to the deceased's home. Here, they have a meal and prayers.

Although Hindu funerals are sorrowful occasions, Hindus avoid extreme mourning. The release of the soul from life is supposed to be a joyous time. Too much sorrow or mourning binds the soul to the Earth, instead of letting it travel on. During the mourning period, friends and relatives visit the family. While they are mourning, the family is "impure." Traditionally, a female widow wears a white sari and removes the red mark on her forehead, placed there at her marriage. During mourning, the family do not join in festivals or other ceremonies.

After the eleventh or thirteenth day after death, Hindus believe that the soul of the dead person has arrived at its destination. To mark the end of this samskar, there is a ceremony called *kriya*. A Brahmin blesses the house and pinda is offered to the deceased, to show the family's thanks for his or her life. After kriya, the mourners continue with their lives. Each year, on the anniversary of the death, the family offers rice balls to the poor in memory of their loved one. This is called *shradh*.

Hindu relatives cook rice balls to give to the poor. Along with showing thanks for the deceased's life, this helps their soul reach its destination in another realm.

28

People often make special journeys to India to scatter the ashes of a loved one in the River Ganges.

Hindus believe that all living things are caught in a continuous cycle of birth and death called *samsara*. When the soul reaches purity and understands true wisdom, it can join Brahman (the ultimate reality from which everything comes and to which it returns). Brahman does not judge the soul. The fate of the soul depends upon a person's actions on Earth.

Good actions or *karma* on Earth determine the fate of a soul in the afterlife, its passage through heaven and its return to Earth in a different physical body. Bad karma determines the soul's fate to lower worlds and hells, and its return to Earth as a "lower" form of life, such as an insect. Returning to Earth in a different physical form is called *reincarnation*. Souls pass through many hundreds of reincarnations before they are released from the cycle. Each time, the soul learns from the experience of heaven and hell, so that that it has better karma in the next reincarnation and eventually finds release, or *moksha*, from the cycle as a truly wise soul.

FOCUS ON:
Yama

Yama is the Hindu god of death. Yama's frightening messengers bring dead souls to appear before Yama in his palace. Here, Yama sits in judgement, hearing about the good and bad actions of the soul on Earth. A soul who has lived reasonably well may be sent back to Earth to take up another physical body. A soul who did not live so well is sent to one of the many Hindu hells, before being sent back to Earth to continue in the cycle of birth, death, and rebirth.

Journeying to God

*S*ikhs, followers of the Sikh religion, sometimes refer to death as a sleep. A person awakes from that sleep in another world. Death is the beginning of a joyous journey toward God. The style of a Sikh funeral reflects this attitude toward death.

FOCUS ON:
The five K's

In 1699, Guru Gobind Singh founded the *Khalsa*, a community of Sikhs who would honor Sikh values. To mark membership of the Khalsa, Sikhs agree to wear the five K's. These are:

Kesh: uncut hair, which symbolizes obedience to God by not interfering with nature. The long hair is wrapped up in a turban.

Kangha: a wooden comb, used to keep the long hair tidy, a symbol of order in life.

Kara: a steel bracelet. Its circular shape stands for the God who has no beginning or end, and the steel represents strength.

Kachera: white shorts worn under clothes. These remind Sikhs of their duty to remain pure and to exercise self-control.

Kirpan: a symbolic short sword that reminds Sikhs always to fight for the truth and defend the weak.

When a Sikh is dying, friends and relatives gather around and offer prayers and readings from the Sikh holy book, the Guru Granth Sahib. The person hears those who are gathered recite the name of *Waheguru*, or Wonderful Lord. Sometimes the dying person drinks some *amrit*, a mixture of sugar and water that has been blessed and stirred with a *khanda*, a double-edged sword.

After death, family members prepare the body for the funeral. Traditionally, they bathe the body with yogurt. As they do this, they recite the *Mool Mantar*, a short verse about the nature of God. The family dresses the body in new clothes and often a new turban. Sikhs who are members of the *Khalsa*—those who have formally taken on the Sikh faith in a ceremony—are prepared with the five K's, the symbols of Sikhism (see box). Then the body is wrapped in a white shroud.

Relatives and friends view the body, either at the home of the deceased or at the gurdwara, the Sikh temple, or place of worship. A special piece of silk called a *rumala* is put over the body. The rumala is usually used to cover the Guru Granth Sahib (see page 35) in the gurdwara.

Traditionally, Sikhs try to cremate the body within 24 hours of death. In some countries this is possible, but in other countries, there may be a delay. Depending on the country where the person dies, cremation takes place either on a funeral pyre or in a crematorium.

Sikh mourners view the body of the deceased before cremation. Sikhs believe the body should be quickly burned so that the soul can journey back to God.

Sacred text

There is One God
Whose Name is True
The Creator
Without fear
Without hate
Immortal
Beyond the cycle
of birth and death
Self-revealing
As Grace.

The Mool Mantar

The funeral service

In some parts of the world, relatives carry the body to the place of cremation. In the funeral procession, people sing *shabads* (hymns from the Guru Granth Sahib), to help the family to contain their sorrow. Even close family and friends try not to show their emotion at the loss of a loved one, because their religion teaches that death is a journey toward God. Sikhs believe that God is inside every person, no matter how bad they seem to be. They believe that everyone can change. Death is not the end: it is the opening to a life of joy in the presence of God.

Men and women wear headscarves. Colorful flowers and wreaths, often in the shape of the Sikh symbol, are placed around the body or coffin. The Sikh symbol is the *khanda*, the double-edged sword that symbolizes the power of God.

Friends sing hymns and recite from the Sikh scriptures. This offers support and comfort to the relatives. A short service before the cremation features sacred hymns and prayers asking for peace for the departed soul, to help the soul become one with God and to be released from the bond of reincarnation.

As friends and relatives carry the body toward the cremation site, they recite hymns that encourage them to accept that death is God's will.

The *Kirtan Sohila*, the Sikh nighttime prayer, is recited. The prayer asks for God's blessing to free the soul from the cycle of death and rebirth, called *mukti*, so that it may pass straight to heaven. Sometimes brief speeches about the deceased are also said. A member of the family (usually the eldest son) lights the fire or pushes the button to start the cremation.

After the cremation, the ashes are scattered in a nearby river. There are no memorial stones because Sikhs believe the body is only a shell, and once the soul has departed, it should not be marked in any way. After the scattering of the ashes, the family arranges for a noncontinuous reading of the Guru Granth Sahib. This is timed so that the reading is completed on the tenth day after the cremation.

Sikhs believe that by burning the body of the deceased, they will encourage the person's soul to leave the body and pass to Heaven.

Sacred text

Death of which men are afraid, gives me nothing but joy! It is through the gate of Death that one may unite with the Lord of Bliss.

Guru Granth Sahib p.1365

Readings and prayers

*A*fter the cremation, friends and family wash their hands and face. Then they go to the family home or the gurdwara to hear poems. They give out *karah parshad*, a sweet food made from flour, semolina, sugar, water, and butter. This is a symbol of God's blessing. Neighbors and friends also prepare food for the bereaved family.

Ten days after the cremation, the family completes the reading of Guru Granth Sahib. The reading reminds friends and family of the deceased of the power of God. When the reading is complete, the *Ardas*, the formal Sikh prayer, is read. Then there is a final reading of a verse taken at random from any page in the Guru Granth Sahib. Karah parshad is given out again. Sometimes the eldest member of the family is given a turban and becomes the new head of the family.

Sikhs believe in reincarnation. Our actions on Earth, or karma, influence the life we are reborn into. A life of prayer and good actions can give a person good karma. This breaks the cycle of rebirth, so that a person's soul can join forever with God.

The Guru Granth Sahib was compiled by Guru Arjan. It is read by relatives of the deceased after the funeral to give them comfort and support.

FOCUS ON:
The Guru Granth Sahib

The Guru Granth Sahib contains 1,430 pages and 3,384 hymns. There is no one spiritual leader in Sikhism. Instead, Sikhs find spiritual wisdom in the Guru Granth Sahib. In the gurdwara, this holy book is the focus of attention. It is placed on a raised platform and covered with a rumala when it is not being read. The Guru Granth Sahib must be placed in its own room. Its presence makes the room or building holy, so any room with the holy book inside is a gurdwara.

The Guru Granth Sahib is kept at the Harmandir Sahib, also known as the Golden Temple, in Amritsar. The temple is the most sacred site for Sikhs.

In the Sikh faith, death is not a sorrowful occasion because it is a doorway to God; emotional anniversaries do not fit in with the Sikh view of death. However, Sikhs observe gurpurbs. These are important anniversaries related to lives of the ten Gurus, or teachers, of the Sikh faith. A gurpurb often features a procession, led by five men wearing yellow robes and turbans. A colorfully decorated float follows behind, carefully carrying the Guru Granth Sahib. Many people join the procession, singing shabads.

A Buddhist funeral

*B*uddhism spread from India to other Southeast Asian countries such as Thailand, Sri Lanka, and Japan. There are many Buddhist traditions, based largely on its geographical spread. Each tradition has different ways of marking a person's death. Today, many more people in Western countries follow the Buddhist philosophy and teachings (*dhamma*, sometimes spelled *dharma*). There are no particular rules or guidelines about the funeral ceremony or other rituals around death. For instance, Buddhists can choose either cremation or burial.

Buddhists do not believe in a soul. They believe that a stream of consciousness, or an "energy," is carried over after death. This is created by a person's actions in life or karma, as well as by his or her last thoughts. A positive and wholesome outlook at death will help to ensure that the transfer of consciousness to a new life is also positive and wholesome. If it is possible, friends, family, and Buddhist monks sit with a person who is dying. Sometimes they read from Buddhist writings or repeat Buddhist *mantras* (phrases). This helps the person to have a peaceful mind; he or she may also wish to meditate to clear the mind.

The Buddhists believe the lotus is a sacred, or holy, flower. It is often used in Buddhist funerals, such as this one where it is used to decorate the coffin.

After death, friends and family view the body, bowing toward it to show respect to the deceased and to acknowledge the impermanent nature of life. Buddhists believe that it takes some time for the "consciousness" to leave the body, so they avoid touching it for at least a few hours after death, or ideally for up to three days. The consciousness is thought to leave through the top of the head. However, Tibetan Buddhists believe that gently touching this part of the body helps to release the consciousness.

People often chant to hold the deceased in mind. The positive thoughts and actions of the living can help the deceased to break free from samsara, the wheel of life, death, and rebirth.

In some parts of Tibet, people choose a sky burial. The body is simply left out on the mountainside. This tradition partly developed because the rocky soil makes burial difficult and there is little wood for cremation. It also developed because Tibetan Buddhists believe that the dead body is merely an empty shell, and it can be put to good use providing food for other animals.

In some parts of Thailand, the body is washed and then placed in a coffin, surrounded by flowers, candles, and incense. Sometimes colored lights decorate the coffin. Before the funeral, neighbors gather for a feast. Monks visit to lead chants. Often, they sit holding a thread attached to the coffin. This helps to transfer good karma from the monks to the deceased. On the day of the funeral, an orchestra plays music to help get rid of any sorrow.

On the day of a Buddhist funeral, the coffin is carried to the funeral site. Monks walk ahead of the coffin and the mourners behind, with male mourners carrying the coffin.

Reaching nirvana

*B*uddhist teaching considers and emphasizes the constantly changing nature of life. This helps Buddhists to understand and face death without fear.

In Buddhism, the transfer of consciousness is likened to a candle flame or spark from one candle to another. The consciousness may be passed on hundreds of times in different bodies. This is sometimes known as rebirth or reincarnation. When a person has achieved total awareness and understanding, he or she is released from samsara, the wheel of birth, death, and rebirth. Release from samsara is *nibanna* or *nirvana*—a state of perfect peace. Buddhism places great emphasis on meditation as a way to uncover a state of heightened awareness.

In Tibetan Buddhism, *bardo* is the state between death and rebirth. Different groups have different ideas about the state of bardo. Most would agree that it lasts 49 days. What happens during this time depends on the level of understanding and awareness that the person achieved during the life that has just ended. A *lama* (teacher) may read prayers and perform ceremonies, which will help the dead person to break free from their old life. Many Tibetan Buddhists believe that relatives can help the person who has died by meditating and carrying out good works. These can be transferred to the person to increase their "merit" (reward for good actions), which will help them to be reborn to a better life.

In some Buddhist traditions, a person's ashes are blessed by monks and then put in a statue of the Buddha or in a stupa (a mound of mud or clay to represent the Buddha's body and enlightened mind). The ashes of the Buddha were distributed under eight stupas.

His Holiness, the 14th Dalai Lama.

The Dalai Lama, the spiritual leader of Tibetan Buddhists, is believed to be the reincarnation of the previous thirteen Dalai Lamas of Tibet (the first was born in 1351 CE). The Dalai Lamas are representations of an enlightened being who chose reincarnation instead of reaching nirvana, in order to serve the people.

Sacred text

Fearing death, I went to the mountains.
Over and over again, I meditated on death's unpredictable coming,
And took the stronghold of the deathless unchanging nature.
Now I am completely beyond all fear of dying!

Milarepa, Tibetan Buddhist monk and poet

Mbuti and humanist rituals

*A*ll over the world, different cultures and communities mark the rite of death in varying ways. These rites may have nothing to do with a particular religion and may only be practiced locally.

Pygmies live in parts of Africa and parts of the Philippines and India. A tribe of pygmies called the Mbuti tribe live as hunter-gatherers in the forests in the Congo. The Mbuti's main belief is in the god of the forest, whose spirit lives in trees and rivers. They perform many ceremonies to worship this god. One of these is the Molimo ritual. This takes place when a bad thing happens, such as a death in the group or a period of poor hunting. The Mbuti believe that the god of the forest is sleeping so they must wake it up.

During the ritual, women and children sit inside their huts, with closed doors. The men gather around a fire, singing and dancing. Some of the younger men go into the forest to collect the molimo, a wooden horn, which hangs from a tree. They wash it in a river, then return to the singing and dancing. Inside the huts, the women listen to the sounds of the forest and of the men, which will waken the forest.

Burial is a simple ceremony, with a grave dug beneath the deceased's hut. After burial, the group often move on and live in another area in the forest.

The Mbuti tribe performing a traditional dance to music.

Humanists have no attachment to religious beliefs. They use their experience and human values to make sense of the world. Humanists believe that there is no life after death. Life is not a preparation for another world. They are concerned with living life well and to the full.

Humanists believe that the dead live on in the memories of the living, through their deeds when they were living, and in their children if they have them. Humanists often plan their funerals in advance.

Humanist funerals respect the nonbelief of the deceased, but also allow religious people to mourn. There are no strict guidelines for a humanist ceremony, but it is likely to include music, readings of literature, spoken memories, and photographs of the deceased. Candles are sometimes lit at a humanist funeral, in memory of the person who has died. Friends and family take time during the funeral to remember the life of the person who has died. There is also usually a period of silence when mourners can reflect on the death in their own way, perhaps by meditation or reflection.

Above all, because a humanist funeral has no religious basis, it is an opportunity for friends and family to remember the person who has died, to celebrate his or her life, and to say goodbye.

FOCUS ON:
Leading a funeral

People who conduct a humanist funeral are called officiants. They are usually trained to lead a humanist funeral and are experienced in dealing with bereavement. Officiants often come from backgrounds that involve caring for or supporting people, such as nursing, teaching, and social work. They are usually over 35 years old and are used to speaking in public.

Sioux and Mexican traditions

There are many different tribes of Native North Americans. Before the white settlers took over their land, they were able to honor the rites of death in traditional ways. Since colonization, they have had to adapt to other ways of living, while still trying to preserve their long-held culture.

The Dakota Indians (or Sioux) of North America have lived along the upper Mississippi Valley and surrounding plains for thousands of years. Traditionally, when tribe members died, there was wailing and mourning. Women cut their arms and legs until they bled. Men smeared their faces with ash. The body was dressed in the person's best clothes and their face painted red, as a symbol of life. It was put on a special platform with the person's favorite things, so that he or she would not have to come back for anything. Bodies were buried in burial mounds.

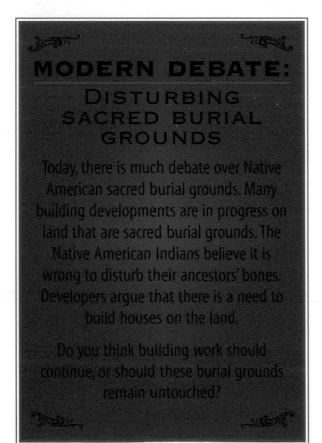

MODERN DEBATE: DISTURBING SACRED BURIAL GROUNDS

Today, there is much debate over Native American sacred burial grounds. Many building developments are in progress on land that are sacred burial grounds. The Native American Indians believe it is wrong to disturb their ancestors' bones. Developers argue that there is a need to build houses on the land.

Do you think building work should continue, or should these burial grounds remain untouched?

The Navajo Indians from the Southwestern United States traditionally burned the house of the deceased. They took the body elsewhere and burned that, too, in the hope that the spirit would not return to haunt them.

In Mexico, the Dia De Los Muertos (Day of the Dead) celebrates the memory of deceased relatives and friends, and invites the souls to return home to hear and enjoy the memories. People clean graves of loved ones and leave food and small offerings for the returning souls. They set up altars in their homes, with photographs of the deceased, and objects that might attract their souls home.

They leave out offerings of small skulls made of sugar and engraved with the name of the deceased. Pillows and blankets are left out, too, so the souls can rest after their long journey. Many people wear skull masks and shells, which clatter together to wake the dead.

Deceased children are remembered on November 1st and adults on November 2nd. November 1st is known as "Dia de los Angelitos" (Day of the Little Angels) and November 2nd as "Dia de los Difuntos" (Day of the Dead).

Relatives carry gifts for the deceased as part of the Day of the Dead procession.

FOCUS ON:
Two traditions meet

Originally, the Day of the Dead festival was based on an Aztec ritual of celebrating children and the dead. When the colonizers arrived from Spain, they brought with them Catholic influences. They wanted to abolish this non-Christian festival, which seemed to mock the dead. The festival continued, however, but as a result of the Catholic influence, today, it is held on All Souls' Day.

Religion and death: a summary

Religion	Preparation	Funeral service
Christianity	Body usually embalmed by undertaker. Body sometimes viewed by relatives at funeral home. Often dressed in best clothes.	Includes music, flowers, and eulogies or readings. Priest or minister leads service. Mourners often wear dark clothes. Hymns are sung.
Judaism	Body ritually prepared by specially trained volunteers (men prepare men, women prepare women). Relatives sit with the body at all times before the funeral. Body dressed in simple shroud. Readings from the Psalms take place over body.	Funeral service led by rabbi. Mourners wear dark clothes and tear a hole in their clothing to show their grief. Prayers and psalms are read during the service.
Islam	Body ritually prepared by close relatives (men prepare men, women prepare women). Body dressed in simple shroud. Prayers read over the body of the deceased.	Service led by imam. Mourners form rows facing Makkah (Mecca) behind prayer leader. Prayers are said for the soul of the deceased. Body faces Makkah within grave.
Hinduism	Relatives help prepare the dying by chanting and reading prayers from the Vedas. Body of the deceased is cleansed and dressed in best clothes surrounded by garlands of flowers.	Prayers are said during funeral by mourners. Liquid ghee thrown onto pyre to make the flames burn fiercely. After cremation, ashes of the deceased are scattered in a holy river.
Sikhism	Close relatives bathe and cleanse body. The body is dressed in new clothes and prepared with the 5 K's for Sikhs who are members of the Khalsa. The body is surrounded by flowers.	Hymns and prayers for the deceased are said and sung during the service. A member of the family, usually the eldest son, lights the fire to begin the cremation. Ashes of the deceased are scattered in a river.
Buddhism	No particular preparations before funeral. Monks and relatives usually chant over body of dead.	Body taken to site of burial or cremation by male mourners. Monks usually lead the funeral procession.

Burial	Cremation	Beliefs	Mourning
Burial in coffin. Headstone erected over grave after funeral.	Only for the Christian denominations Anglican and Roman Catholic, but Roman Catholic ashes must be buried.	Belief in eternal life, because of Jesus Christ's sacrifice on the cross. Soul passes to heaven or hell.	Reception after funeral. No formal mourning period. Relatives often lay flowers on grave.
Burial in simple pine coffin or body buried without a coffin. A simple tombstone.	Only for some denominations of Judaism.	Belief in afterlife. Afterlife beliefs differ between Orthodox and Liberal Jews.	Meal after funeral. Mourning period for close family divided into stages of seven days, one month, and 11 months. Prayers on anniversary of death.
Burial in simple pine coffin or burial without a coffin. A plain tombstone.	No cremation for Muslims.	Belief in eternal life—each person called to account at the Last Judgement.	Three-day mourning with increased prayer and devotion. Open expressions of grief are frowned upon.
No burial, all Hindus are cremated.	On a funeral pyre or in a crematorium.	Soul passes to heaven or hell and is then reborn in another body.	Widow wears white sari for 11 or 13 days of mourning. Kriya ceremony marks end of mourning.
No burial, all Sikhs are cremated.	Either on funeral pyre or in a crematorium.	Pure soul is released from cycle of life and rebirth and joins Brahman—the ultimate reality.	No mourning period, but for 10 days relatives read noncontinuous reading of Guru Granth Sahib.
Some Buddhists buried. Sky burial in parts of Tibet.	Some Buddhists cremated. Ashes sometimes blessed by monks.	Rebirth as transfer of consciousness from one body to another. Nirvana reached when consciousness has total enlightenment.	No formal method of mourning. Relatives encouraged to perform good deeds and think good thoughts so deceased may be reborn to a better life.

Glossary

afterlife life after death

bereaved family and friends of the deceased

brahmin member of the priestly caste or group

cemetery place where bodies are buried

consecrated made holy

corpse dead body

cremation process of burning dead bodies

crematorium building where dead bodies are burned

deceased dead person

denomination branch of a religion that shares core beliefs but has some different interpretations or ways of worshiping

embalm to preserve a body for a while and make it look more lifelike

enlightenment in Buddhism a state of "awakening," or understanding the true nature of the universe

epitaph inscription on a tombstone

eulogy speech that remembers a person who has died

ghee liquid part of butter that has been melted and chilled, so the liquid can be separated

gurdwara Sikh place of worship

Holy Communion sacrament in which bread and wine are taken as reminders of the last meal of Jesus Christ, and of his death

imam Muslim prayer leader

immortal never dies

meditation sitting quietly to clear the mind

mosque Islamic place of worship

mourner person grieving at the death of a loved one

priest person who has been ordained (consecrated) so that they can lead services in the Christian Church

Protestant branch of Christianity that is separate from Roman Catholicism and Eastern Orthodoxy

pyre pile of wood used for burning a dead body

rabbi Jewish spiritual leader

realm other world

reincarnation belief that after death, a person's soul lives in another body

repent say sorry

resurrection rising from the dead

rite ceremony

rite of passage ceremony to mark an important stage in a person's life, such as birth, marriage, and death

ritual ceremony following a set series of actions

Roman Catholic branch of Christianity that recognizes the Pope as its religious authority

Sabbath Jewish religious day of rest and worship

sacred holy or worthy of religious respect

sin wrongdoing

soul person's spirit

synagogue Jewish place of worship

undertaker person who undertakes much of the organization of a funeral

wake meeting before (or sometimes after) a funeral to celebrate the dead person's life

Find out more and Web Sites

Books

Living Religions: Living Buddhism
Cavan Wood (Raintree, 2003)

Living Religions: Living Christianity
Lynne Gibson (Raintree, 2003)

Living Religions: Living Judaism
Cavan Wood (Raintree, 2003)

Living Religions: Living Sikhism
Jon Mayled (Raintree, 2003)

Religions of the World: The Illustrated Guide to Origins, Beliefs, Customs, and Festivals
Elizabeth Breuilly (Checkmark Books, 2005)

The Kids Book of World Religions
Jennifer Glossop (Kids Can Press, 2003)

The Time of Our Lives: A Teen Guide to the Jewish Life Cycle
Scott Blumenthal (Berhman House, 2003)

Web Sites

Due to the changing nature of Internet links, Rosen Publishing has developed an online list of Web sites related to the subject of this book. This site is regularly updated. Please use this link to access this list: www.rosenlinks.com/jol/death

TEACHER NOTES

- Find out where your nearest cemetery is and plan to visit. Look at the gravestones and the different memorial stones. What do they tell you about the person and his or her faith?

- Research the internet for details of the funeral or burial of a famous person (choose one follower of each of the main religions).

- Make up a list of local Buddhist monasteries, Hindu temples, Islamic mosques, Sikh gurdwaras, Christian churches, and Jewish synagogues. Plan to visit one of them.

- Ask an older relative or friend of the family to tell you how people marked death 50 years ago. How has it changed from today?

- Ask an imam, a rabbi, a priest, a member of the Khalsa, a Buddhist monk or nun, or a Hindu priest to visit the school, and discuss with them how they mark death in their religion.

- Research novels that feature funerals and burials. Can you find references to at least four of the main religions' funeral practices?

Index